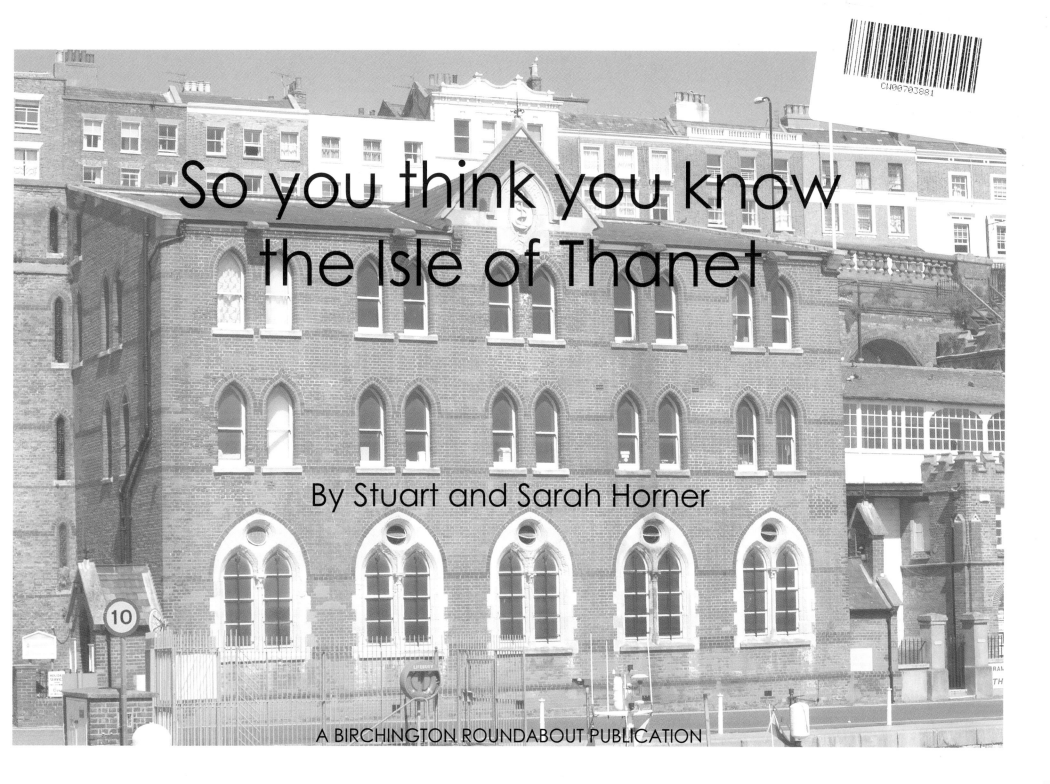

So you think you know the Isle of Thanet

By Stuart and Sarah Horner

A BIRCHINGTON ROUNDABOUT PUBLICATION

Contents

Introduction   4

The collection of photographs   5

Index of locations   85

Contact details for more information about Thanet   95

Help Captain Thanet fun page!   96

Introduction

Though we were both born on the Isle of Thanet and have lived and worked here most of our lives, we thought we knew the area fairly well. Yet when it came to photographing Thanet's unusual buildings, curious details and land marks we had to admit to being stunned by the variety and beauty around us. Without close scrutiny these features had blended into the back ground and when the camera zoomed in they literally came back into focus.

Some of the pictures celebrate the overall beauty of Thanet, whilst others highlight the delightful details which seem so familiar, yet may be difficult to place. The joy of this project was capturing an alternative view of Thanet which has caused us to look more closely at the obscure, a little longer at the familiar and discovering by chance a further dimension.

The book is rather like a jigsaw puzzle. When all of the pieces are identified and finally locked together they reveal a wonderful overall impression of The Isle of Thanet. We hope this will encourage visitors and residents alike to seek out more information and undertake deeper investigation into the heart of Thanet using these contemporary pictures as a slightly unconventional guide book.

Stuart and Sarah Horner
September 2007

10

11

12

13

14

15

16

17

18

19

20

21

22

24

23

25

26

28

11

31

32

33

37

38

39

40

41

42

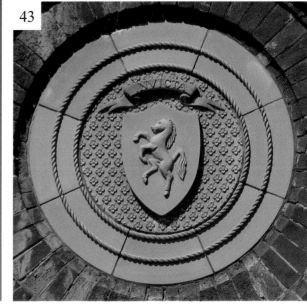

43

44

45

46

47

48

49

50

55

57

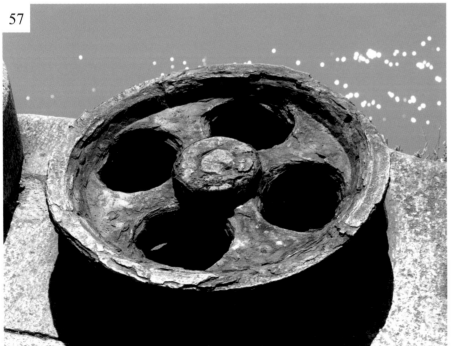

56

TIME FLIES
VIRTUE ALONE REMAINS

58

59

60

61

62

66

67

68

21

69

71

72

70

73

74

75

76

77

23

78

79

80

81

82

83

91

92

93

94

96

97

101

102

103

104

106

105

107

108

109

110

111

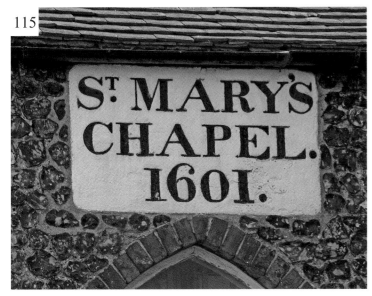

115

116

117

118

120

119

121

122

123

124

125

126

127

128

129

130

131

132

133

134

135

136

137

138

139

140

141

142

143

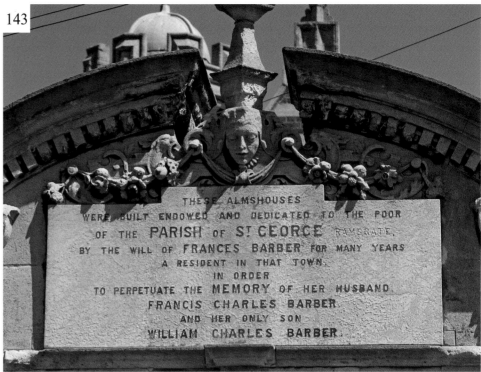

THESE ALMSHOUSES
WERE BUILT ENDOWED AND DEDICATED TO THE POOR
OF THE PARISH of St GEORGE RAMSGATE.
BY THE WILL OF FRANCES BARBER FOR MANY YEARS
A RESIDENT IN THAT TOWN.
IN ORDER
TO PERPETUATE THE MEMORY OF HER HUSBAND.
FRANCIS CHARLES BARBER.
AND HER ONLY SON
WILLIAM CHARLES BARBER.

144

147

148

149

150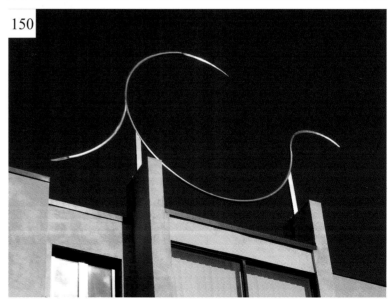

151

152

153

154

155

156

157

158

159

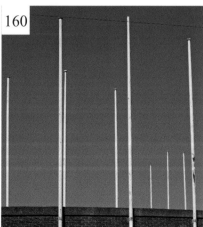

160

161

162

163

164

165

166

168

167

169

170

171

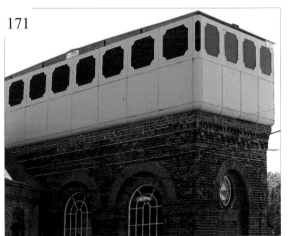

172

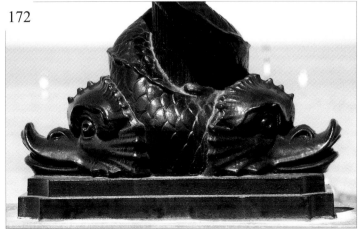

173

174

175

176

177

178

179

182

180

181

51

183

184

185

186

187

188

189

190

191

192

193

54

194

195

196

55

197

198

199 WES

200

201

202

203

204

205

206

207

208

209

210

211

212

213

214

215

216

217

218

219

220

221

222

223

224

225

226

227

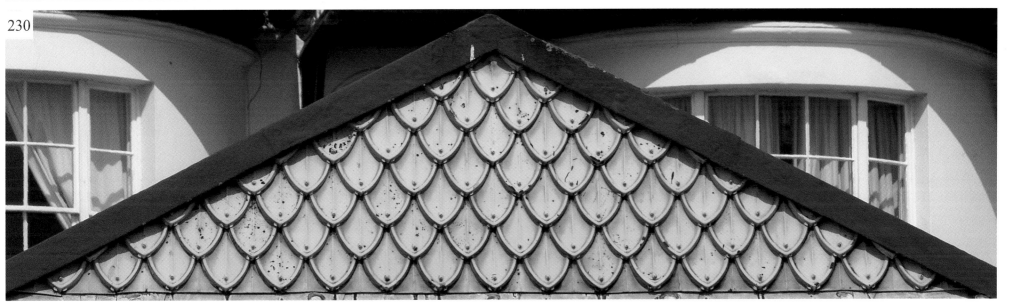

63

231

232

233

234

235

236

237

238

239

240

241

242

243

244

245

246

247

248

249

250

251

252

253

254

255

256

257

258

261

259

260

262

263

264

265

266

267

268

269

270

271

272

273

275

274

276

279

282

277

280

278

281

283

284

285

286

287

288

289

IN
MEMORY
OF
NINE HEROIC MEN
WHO LOST THEIR LIVES BY
CAPSIZING OF THE
MARGATE SURF BOAT
"FRIEND TO ALL NATIONS"
IN ATTEMPTING
TO ASSIST A VESSEL IN DISTRESS AT
2ND DEC. 1897.

290

291

292

NORTHUMBERLAND
HALL.

293

294

295

296

297

298

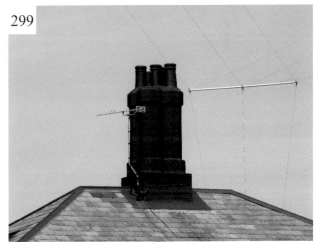

299

300

301

302

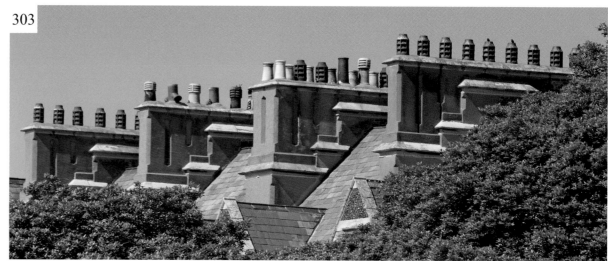

303

304

305

306

307

308

309

310

311

RESCUE

312

313

316

PINEAPPLE
HOUSE

314

315

317

318

321

319

320

322

323

324

325

326

327

328

329

330

333

331

332
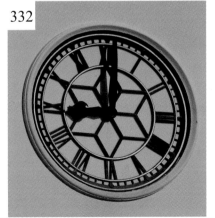

334

335

336

337

339

338

Photo No.   Location

1   The Spread Eagle public house, Victoria Road, Margate.
2   Lamp post, Marine Terrace, Margate.
3   Sailors' Chapel, Military Road, Royal harbour, Ramsgate.
4   Shelter, Marine Terrace, Margate.
5   Former Royal Sea Bathing Hospital, Canterbury Road, Westbrook, Margate.
6   Rear of The Palace Cinema, Harbour Street, Broadstairs.
7   Clock Tower, Marine Terrace, Margate.
8   Broadstairs train station, High Street, Broadstairs.
9   Tudor House, King Street, Margate.
10   Margate Language Centre, Churchfield Place, Hawley Square, Margate.
11   Granville House, Victoria Parade, Ramsgate.
12   Crampton Tower, The Broadway, Broadstairs.
13   Corner of Harbour Parade and Kent Terrace, Ramsgate.
14   Chimney pots, Madeira Walk, Ramsgate.
15   Chimney pots opposite Kingsgate Bay, Broadstairs.
16   Chimney below Marina Road, Ramsgate.
17   Beacon, Stone Pier, Margate harbour.
18   Chimney above 19 St Mildred's Road, Westgate.
19   Clock Tower, Marine Terrace, Margate.
20   John Sanger's memorial, Margate cemetery, Manston Road.
21   Marks & Spencer, Westwood Cross Shopping Centre, Broadstairs.
22   Harbour Parade, Ramsgate.
23   Debenhams, Westwood Cross Shopping Centre, Broadstairs.
24   Above 75-85 Northdown Road, Cliftonville.
25   Roof of The Foy Boat public house, Sion Hill, Ramsgate.
26   Gate to George VI Memorial Park, Montefiore Avenue, Ramsgate.
27   Clock near entrance to Margate cemetery, Manston Road, Margate.
28   All Saints Church, All Saints Avenue, Margate.
29   Margate train station, off Marine Terrace, Margate.
30   The Lido, Ethelbert Terrace, Cliftonville.
31   North Foreland Lighthouse, North Foreland Road, Broadstairs.
32   Bethesda Medical Centre, Palm Bay Avenue, Cliftonville.
33   Former Flour Mill, Margate Road, Ramsgate.

34   All Saints' Church, Canterbury Road, Birchington.

35   Italianate greenhouse, King George VI Memorial Park, Montefiore Avenue, Ramsgate.

36   Bandstand, Wellington Crescent, Ramsgate.

37   Water Board building, Manston Road, between Birchington and Manston.

38   St Catherine's Church, Manston.

39   Italianate greenhouse, King George VI Memorial Park, Montefiore Avenue, Ramsgate.

40   Sign at junction of College Road, (Victoria traffic lights), Margate.

41   Dent-de-Lion, Dent-de-Lion Road, Garlinge.

42   Fountain at Dane Park, Margate.

43   Medallion on arches at Military Road, Ramsgate Royal harbour.

44   Shelter in Victoria Gardens, Victoria Parade, Broadstairs.

45   The Shopping Centre, Margate.

46   Emblem over arches, Military Road, Ramsgate Royal harbour.

47   Tribute to Unknown Airmen, RAF History Museum, Manston Road, Manston.

48   St Mary Magdalene Church, Monkton Street, Monkton.

49   Sarre Windmill, Sarre.

50   Former church, Cavendish Street, Ramsgate.

51   Former home for smack boys, Military Road, Ramsgate Royal harbour.

52   Harbour office on the jetty, Broadstairs.

53   St Joseph's Primary School, St Peters Park Road, Broadstairs.

54   QEQM hospital, St Peters Road, Margate.

55   St Paul's Church, Northdown Road, Cliftonville.

56   Montefiore Synagogue, Honeysuckle Lane, Ramsgate.

57   Pulley wheel, west pier, Ramsgate Royal harbour.

58   Viaduct, Margate Road, Ramsgate.

59   Above 2, Charlotte Street, Broadstairs.

60   Clock, Old Town Hall, Market Place, Margate.

61   Former police station, Cavendish Street, Ramsgate.

62   33a High Street, St Lawrence, Ramsgate.

63   Former water tower, Southwood Road, Ramsgate.

64   Margate Mosque, Union Crescent, Margate.

65   St Thomas' Church, Minnis Road, Birchington.

66   Bandstand, Ellington Park, Ramsgate.

67   Customs House, Harbour Parade, Ramsgate.

68   Shaw's lighthouse, west pier, Ramsgate Royal harbour.

69	Weather vane on Post Office, Cecil Square, Margate.
70	St George's Church, Church Road, Ramsgate.
71	Sign on side of S H Cuttings, Market Place, Margate.
72	The White Swan public house, Reading Street, Broadstairs.
73	World War I memorial, Lewis Crescent, Cliftonville.
74	Cooling towers at Richborough, as seen from Ramsgate harbour.
75	188 High Street, Margate.
76	Cliff top, Grenham Bay, Birchington.
77	Drapers Homes, (Yoakley Charity), St Peters Road, Margate.
78	Water tower, Rumfields Road, Broadstairs.
79	St Augustine's Cross, Cottington Road, Cliffsend, Ramsgate.
80	Chimney in Albion Road, St Peters, Broadstairs.
81	Shelter, Queen's Promenade, Cliftonville.
82	The Lido, Ethelbert Terrace, Cliftonville.
83	Bandstand, Eastern Esplanade, Cliftonville.
84	Comfort Inn, Victoria Parade, Ramsgate.
85	Chimney at West Cliff Mews, West Cliff Road, Broadstairs.
86	SS Austin and Gregory Church, Victoria Road, Margate.
87	Buckmaster House Residential Home, Western Esplanade, Broadstairs.
88	The Shopping Centre, Margate.
89	Entrance to The Grange (Pugin's House), St Augustine's Road, Ramsgate.
90	Sgraffito decoration on Sunny Lodge, Spencer Road, Birchington.
91	Clock on 69 High Street, Broadstairs.
92	1 Ethelbert Terrrace, Westgate.
93	The 'Hugin' Viking Ship, Sandwich Road, Pegwell Bay, Ramsgate.
94	Harbour office on the jetty, Broadstairs.
95	Margate sea front.
96	St Andrew's Church, Reading Street, Broadstairs.
97	Fire Station, Effingham Street, Ramsgate.
98	Marine Terrace and beach, Margate.
99	Lift at Viking Bay, Broadstairs.
100	Cliffs at Dumpton Gap, Broadstairs.
101	50 Harbour Parade, Ramsgate.
102	51 Albion Street, Broadstairs.
103	Wishing Towers, Eastern Esplanade, Cliftonville.

69

83

93

104   Corner of Chatham Street and High Street, Ramsgate.
105   Westgate Library, Minster Road, Westgate.
106   Memorial to surf boat disaster, Marine Terrace, Margate.
107   Former Motor Museum, Paragon, Ramsgate.
108   Scenic Railway, Dreamland site, Margate.
109   Police Station, 54 High Street, Broadstairs.
110   2 Duke Street, Margate.
111   The Bull's Head public house, Market Street, Margate.
112   Drapers Homes, St Peters Road, Margate.
113   St John the Baptist Church, Churchfields, Margate.
114   Tom Thumb Theatre, Eastern Esplanade, Cliftonville.
115   St Mary's Chapel, 44 Albion Street, Broadstairs.
116   Fountain, Dane Park, Margate.
117   Above 1 High Street, Broadstairs.
118   30 Harbour Street, Ramsgate.
119   Shaw's Lighthouse, west pier, Ramsgate Royal harbour.
120   Steps on west pier, Ramsgate Royal harbour.
121   5a Station Road, Westgate.
122   Site of first telephone cable to France, Dumpton Gap, Broadstairs.
123   Clock Tower, Marine Terrace, Margate.
124   Northdown House, Northdown Park Road, Cliftonville.
125   Fountain, Dane Park, Margate.
126   Corner of High Street and The Parade, Margate.
127   Above Nationwide, 52-54 High Street, Ramsgate.
128   Emblem on former hospital, West Cliff Road, Ramsgate.
129   Above 4 High Street, Broadstairs.
130   Queen's Head public house, Harbour Parade, Ramsgate.
131   Old Town Hall, Market Place, Margate.
132   Charles Dickens, Bleak House, Fort Road, Broadstairs.
133   The Prince Albert Public house, 38 High Street, Broadstairs.
134   Lloyds TSB bank, 9 Queen Street, Ramsgate.
135   Statue of Sir Erasmus Wilson at former Royal Sea Bathing Hospital, Margate.
136   Ornate headstone, Margate cemetery.
137   Detail on the Clock Tower, Marine Terrace, Margate.
138   View of windmills from Acol.

139   Detail on St Augustine's Church, St Augustine's Road, Ramsgate.
140   Winterstoke Gardens, Victoria Parade, Ramsgate.
141   Beacon at Margate harbour, looking towards Westbrook.
142   Entrance to outer harbour, Ramsgate.
143   Gateway to Almshouses, Elms Avenue, Ramsgate.
144   Sunny Lodge, Spencer Road, Birchington.
145   The Grange (Pugin's house), St Augustine's Road, Ramsgate.
146   War memorial, The Square, Birchington.
147   Carlton Cinema, St Mildred's Road, Westgate.
148   Corner of Percy Road and Sweyn Road, Cliftonville.
149   Opposite corner of Percy Road and Sweyn Road, Cliftonville.
150   Above new flats in Fort Road, Margate.
151   Transmitter tower, North Foreland Lighthouse, North Foreland Road, Broadstairs.
152   Drapers Mill, St Peters Footpath, Margate.
153   Nuckell's Alms House, High Street, St Peters, Broadstairs.
154   Side of 46 High Street, Broadstairs.
155   Drapers Homes, St Peters Road, Margate.
156   St Mary's Church, Church Street, Minster.
157   The Pavillion, Harbour Street, Broadstairs.
158   Window below water tank, Margate train station.
159   Above Top Shop, Westwood Cross Shopping Centre, Broadstairs.
160   Flag poles, The Shopping Centre, Margate.
161   Kingsgate Castle, Joss Gap Road, Broadstairs.
162   St Nicholas Church, St Nicholas at Wade.
163   2 Cecil Square, Margate.
164   Our Lady and St Benedict Church, Minnis Road, Birchington.
165   Memorial to Dante Gabriel Rossetti, Sandles Road, Birchington.
166   The Wig and Pen public house, Market Place, Margate.
167   Shopping parade, Station Road, Westgate.
168   Burma Star Memorial, Trinity Square, Margate.
169   Gate to St Mary Magdalene Church yard, Monkton Street, Monkton.
170   Royal Parade, Ramsgate.
171   Water tank, Margate train station.
172   Lamp post, Marine Terrace, Margate (see also picture 2).
173   25 and 27 High Street, Ramsgate.

174   Above NatWest Bank, 53 High Steet, Ramsgate.

175   Steps at Viking Bay, Broadstairs.

176   Statue at College Square Shopping Centre, Margate.

177   Corner of Northdown Road and Cliftonville Avenue, Cliftonville.

178   Kennedy House, Plains of Waterloo, Ramsgate.

179   Drapers Homes, St Peters Road, Margate (see also picture 112).

180   The 'Hugin' Viking Ship, Sandwich Road, Ramsgate.

181   St Paul's Church, Northdown Road, Cliftonville.

182   Pierremont Hall, High Street, Broadstairs.

183   Gates to St George's Church, Church Road, Ramsgate.

184   Seats adjacent to Winterstoke Gardens, Victoria Parade, Ramsgate.

185   Pegwell Bay Hotel, Pegwell Road, Ramsgate.

186   The Lido, Ethelbert Terrace, Cliftonville.

187   Montefiore Synagogue, Honeysuckle Lane, Ramsgate.

188   Top of lift, Madeira Walk, Ramsgate.

189   Carlton Cinema, St Mildred's Road, Westgate (see picture 147).

190   Ornate headstone, Margate cemetery.

191   Ramsgate train station.

192   Former gas works office, Boundary Road, Ramsgate.

193   Stone Pier at Margate harbour.

194   Droit House, Margate harbour.

195   York Gate, Harbour Street, Broadstairs.

196   Charleston Court, West Cliff Road, Broadstairs.

197   Lady Star of the Sea Church, Broadstairs Road, Broadstairs.

198   Stocks at St Mary Magdelene Church, Monkton Street, Monkton.

199   Wall tiling, Westgate Library, Minster Road, Westgate.

200   Lamp-posts at Westbrook Promenade, behind Nayland Rock Hotel, Margate.

201   St Anne's Church, Eastern Esplanade, Cliftonville.

202   Summerlands Lodge, Canterbury Road, Westgate.

203   Ships anchor in wall around Bleak House, Fort Road, Broadstairs.

204   Lloyds TSB bank, 42 High Street, Broadstairs.

205   Medallion on Margate train station.

206   Wall light, Morelli's, 14 Victoria Parade, Broadstairs.

207   Former Flour Mill, Margate Road, Ramsgate.

208   Corner of Harbour Parade and Madeira Walk, Ramsgate.

209   Chimney on corner of Royal Crescent, St Augustine's Road, Ramsgate.
210   Scenic Railway, Dreamland site, Margate.
211   The Waverley public house, The Parade, Margate.
212   51 Queen Street, Ramsgate.
213   Below Winterstoke Gardens, Victoria Parade, Ramsgate.
214   Chapel, Former Royal Sea Bathing Hospital, Canterbury Road, Margate.
215   The 'Hugin' Viking Ship, Sandwich Road, Ramsgate.
216   Chatham House Grammar School, Chatham Street, Ramsgate.
217   St Mary's Church, Church Street, Minster.
218   Statue on Casino, The Pavillion, Harbour Parade, Ramsgate.
219   Marine Sands Restaurant, adjacent to the clock tower, Margate.
220   John Sanger's memorial, Margate cemetery, Manston Road, Margate.
221   Masonic Lodge, New Cross Street, Margate.
222   The Alexandra Homes, Tivoli Road, Margate.
223   Bust of Edward Welby Pugin (Son of Augustus Pugin), Victoria Parade, Ramsgate.
224   Station Road, Westgate (see also picture 167).
225   The Baptist Church, New Street, Margate.
226   Our Lady and St Benedict Church, Minnis Road, Birchington.
227   Kingsgate Bay, Broadstairs.
228   Minster Abbey, Church Street, Minster.
229   St Mildred's Church, Plumstone Road, Acol.
230   The Pavillion, Harbour Street, Broadstairs.
231   Margate Adult Education Centre, Hawley Square, Margate.
232   Rooftops from Madeira Walk, Ramsgate.
233   Derelict studio of Soloman J Soloman set in cliff near Epple Bay, Birchington.
234   Broadstairs Parish Church of Holy Trinity, Church Road, Broadstairs.
235   Above Next, Westwood Cross Shopping Centre, Broadstairs.
236   Wind turbine, Richborough, Nr Ramsgate.
237   Jacob's Ladder steps between Royal Parade and Military Road, Ramsgate harbour.
238   Above Alexandra Restaurant, Harbour Parade, Ramsgate.
239   Period detail on corner of Victoria Parade and Albert Road, Ramsgate.
240   The New Inn, New Street, Margate.
241   Theatre Royal, Addington Street, Margate.
242   The Salvation Army Citadel, Union Crescent, Margate.
243   Searchlight, RAF History Museum, Manston Road, Manston.

208

218

230

244	Sculpture at Westwood Cross Shopping Centre, Broadstairs.
245	Lamp on Harbour Office, the jetty, Broadstairs harbour.
246	Top of lift at West Cliff Promende, Ramsgate.
247	Plaque over toilets at Harbour Street, Broadstairs.
248	West Cliff Park, Royal Esplanade, Ramsgate.
249	Surf boat memorial, Margate Cemetery, Margate.(see photograph 289)
250	Horse trough and drinking fountain, The Square, Birchington.
251	Corner of St Mildred's Road and Cuthbert Road, Westgate.
252	Lorry park, Ramsgate harbour ferry terminal.
253	St Augustine's conference centre, Canterbury Road, Westgate.
254	Methodist Church, Canterbury Road, Birchington.
255	Bollard on east pier, Ramsgate Royal harbour.
256	52 Northdown Road, Cliftonville.
257	Christ Church United Reformed Church, Westgate Bay Avenue, Westgate.
258	Fleete Pumping Station, Manston Court Road, Manston.
259	Obelisk to George IV's visit in 1821, Harbour Parade, Ramsgate.
260	Roof of staircase to Winter Gardens, Fort Crescent, Margate.
261	39 Harbour Street, Ramsgate.
262	Plane at Manston Road, Manston.
263	Canon at Fort Crescent, Margate.
264	Carlton Cinema, St Mildred's Road, Westgate.
265	Stone lion in Kingsgate Bay Road, Broadstairs.
266	Walkway overlooking Fort Lower Promenade, above Winter Gardens, Margate.
267	Shelter at top of Fort Hill, Margate.
268	Detail at Margate train Station.
269	Gasometer between Boundary Road and St Luke's Avenue, Ramsgate.
270	11 Broad Street, Margate.
271	Side of NatWest Bank, 47 High Street, Broadstairs.
272	Maritime Museum, Harbour Parade, Ramsgate.
273	Shelter at Victoria Gardens, Victoria Parade, Broadstairs.
274	Cecil Square Baptist Church, Cecil Square, Margate.
275	Corner of Northdown Road and Lyndhurst Avenue, Cliftonville.
276	Control tower, Kent International Airport, Manston.
277	Rising pontoon at Ramsgate Royal harbour.
278	HM Coastguard, Palm Bay Avenue, Cliftonville.

253

272

273

279 Chimney above Nationwide, 52-54 High Street, Ramsgate.
280 The Waterloo Tower, Quex Park, Birchington.
281 Clock on shelter, Victoria Gardens, Broadstairs (see picture 273).
282 Brickwork on St Edmunds (next to Pugin's House), St Augustine's Road, Ramsgate.
283 Marks & Spencer, Westwood Cross Shopping Centre, Broadstairs.
284 Edith Court, former Margate hospital, Victoria Road, Margate.
285 Tudor House, King Street, Margate.
286 Trinity Square, Margate.
287 Former bank building on corner of King Street and Fort Road, Margate.
288 Lift at West Cliff Promenade, Ramsgate.
289 Surf boat memorial, Margate Cemetery, Manston Road, Margate.
290 Westcliff Leisure Park, Royal Esplanade, Ramsgate.
291 Steps adjacent to Kent Terrace, Ramsgate.
292 Northumberland Hall, 39 Northdown Road, Cliftonville.
293 Theatre Royal, Addington Street, Margate.
294 Customs House, Royal Parade, Ramsgate.
295 Above Natwest, 13 Cecil Square, Margate.
296 'Destiny', World War I memorial, Madeira Walk, Ramsgate.
297 Chapel at Ramsgate Cemetery, Cecilia Road, Ramsgate.
298 Doorway, Fort Paragon, Margate.
299 Chimney on house at North Foreland Lighthouse, Broadstairs.
300 Stone Pier at Margate harbour.
301 Gatehouse to Ramsgate Cemetery, Cecilia Road, Ramsgate.
302 Almshouses, Elms Avenue, Ramsgate.
303 Chimneys at Chartham Terrace, St Augustine's Road, Ramsgate.
304 Restaurant at end of Ramsgate harbour wall.
305 Water fall at Madeira Walk, Ramsgate.
306 Royal Albion Hotel, Albion Street, Broadstairs.
307 Corner of Kent Place and Royal Parade, Ramsgate.
308 Lloyds TSB Bank, 42 High Street, Broadstairs.
309 Stone Lion, Victoria Parade, Ramsgate.
310 St Saviour's Church, Westgate Bay Avenue, Westgate.
311 Rescue centre, Ramsgate sands.
312 Christchurch, Vale Square, Ramsgate.
313 Above 231 -241 Northdown Road, Cliftonville.

321   8 King Street, Margate.
322   Clarendon House Grammar School, Clarendon Gardens, Ramsgate.
323   Doorway in Fort Road, Margate.
324   Side of Albion House, Albion Place, Ramsgate.
325   Drapers Homes, St Peters Road, Margate.
326   Entrance to Granville House, Victoria Parade, Ramsgate.
327   14 Albion Street, Broadstairs.
328   St Augustine's Church, St Augustine's Road, Ramsgate.
329   Former Church, 11 Hawley Square, Margate.
330   Top of Clarendon House Grammar School, Clarendon Gardens, Ramsgate.
331   Top of 8 King Street, Margate.
332   Clock face on Droit House, Margate harbour.
333   Corner of Zion Place and Northdown Road, Cliftonville.
334   Christ Church united Reformed Church, Westgate Bay Avenue, Westgate.
335   Chimney at 2 Cuthbert Road, Westgate.
336   Dante Gabriel Rossetti Grave Stone, All Saints Churchyard, Birchington.
337   Brick chimney flu at Royal Crescent, St Augustine's Road, Ramsgate.
338   Plumb Pudding Island, Minnis Bay, Birchington. (Below)Panorama of Minnis Bay looking East
339   Coast Guard Cottages, Victoria Parade, Ramsgate.

More information about The Isle of Thanet is available from the following:

Tourism Service Thanet District Council PO Box 9 Cecil Street, Margate, Kent CT9 1XZ Tel: 01843 577671
e-mail: tourism@thanet.gov.uk

Broadstairs Tourist Information Centre 6B High Street, Broadstairs Tel: 01843 862242 e-mail: tourism@thanet.gov.uk

Broadstairs Visitor Information Centre Dickens House Museum, 2 Victoria Parade, Broadstairs, Kent Tel: 0870 264 6111

Ramsgate Tourist/Visitor Information Centre 17 Albert Ct, York St, Ramsgate 01843 583333 e-mail: ramsgatevic@yahoo.co.uk

Margate Tourist/Visitor Information Centre 12-13 The Parade, Margate, Kent Tel: 0870 264 6111

Beach information - Margate Thanet Coast Line Tel: 0870 264 6111

Harbour information - Ramsgate, Margate, Broadstairs 01843 572100

Thanet cemeteries 01843 224492

Ramsgate Maritime Museum East Kent Maritime Trust, Clock House, Royal Harbour, Ramsgate, Kent. CT11 8LS Tel; 01843 570622

Margate Museum The Old Town Hall, Market Place, Margate CT9 1ER Tel: (01843) 231213

RAF Manston History Museum Manston Road, Ramsgate, Kent Tel: 01843 825224

Tudor House Margate - Guided tours by prior arrangement 01843 231213

The Grange (Augustus Welby Pugin's House) Ramsgate Tel: 01628 825925

Italianate Green House Tel: 01843 585588

North Foreland Lighthouse contact Trinity House, Tower Hill, London Tel: 020 7481 6900

St Augustines Cross Tel: 0870 264 6111

Draper's Windmill Tel: 01843 226227

www.ramsgate-society.org.uk

For our sharp-eyed younger readers?

Can you help Captain Thanet count how many of these are in the book?

Clock faces

Stone lions

Animals
(No real seagulls or pigeons!)

Beards and moustaches

Church spires

Aeroplanes

Parts of a dragon

Flag poles

Weather vanes

Crabs

Bells

Cannons

Answers: 30 clock faces - 16 Bells - 2 Dragon parts - 2 Aeroplanes - 27 Weather vanes - 7 Stone Lions - 8 Beards and moustaches - 1 Cannon - 23 Church spires - 10 flag poles - 20 Animals - 1 Crab